# ENCYCLOPEDIA

# OF A

# BROKEN HEART

ALSO BY JON LUPIN

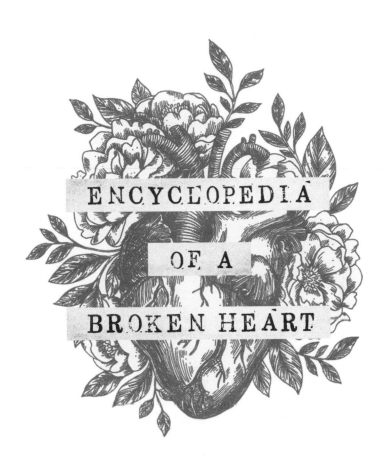

# ENCYCLOPEDIA
## OF A
## BROKEN HEART

JON LUPIN
THE POETRY BANDIT

CASTLE POINT BOOKS
NEW YORK

www.castlepointbooks.com

The Castle Point Books trademark is owned by Castle
Point Publishing, LLC. Castle Point books are published
and distributed by St. Martin's Press.

ISBN 978-1-250-22864-2 (trade paperback)
ISBN 978-1-250-22865-9 (ebook)

Images used under license by Shutterstock.com

Our books may be purchased in bulk for promotional,
educational, or business use. Please contact your local
bookseller or the Macmillan Corporate and Premium
Sales Department at 1-800-221-7945, extension 5442, or
by email at MacmillanSpecialMarkets@macmillan.com.

First Edition: October 2019

10 9 8 7 6 5 4 3 2 1

To those who need
healing or have healed,
this is for you.

# CONTENTS

1
Preface

3
Encyclopedia of a Broken Heart

183
About the Author

bringing to light of the devotion. Ascetic writers spoke of it, especially those of the Society of Jesus, Alvarez de Paz, Luis de la Puente, Saint-Jure, and Nouet, and there still exist special treatises upon it, such as Father Druzbicki's (d. 1662) small work, "Meta Cordium, Cor Jesu". Amongst the mystics and pious souls who practised the devotion were St. Francis Borgia, Blessed Peter Canisius, St. Aloysius Gonzaga, and St. Alphonsus Rodriguez, of the Society of Jesus, the Venerable Marina de Escobar (d. 1633), in Spain, the Venerable Madeleine of St. Joseph and the Venerable Marguerite of the Blessed Sacrament, Carmelites, in France; Jeanne de St. Mathieu Deleloe (d. 1660), a Benedictine, in Belgium, the worthy Armelle of Vannes (d. 1671), and even in Jansenistic or semi-Jansenistic circles, Marie de Valernod (d. 1630) and Angélique Arnauld; M. Boudon, the great archdeacon of Evreux, Father Huby, the apostle of retreats in Brittany, and, above all, the Venerable Marie de l'Incarnation, who died at Quebec in 1672. The Visitation seemed to be awaiting Blessed Margaret Mary; its spirituality, certain intuitions of St. Francis de Sales, the meditations of Mère l'Huillier (d. 1655), the visions of Mother Anne-Marguerite Clément (d. 1661), and of Sister Jeanne-Bénigne Gojoz (d. 1692), all paved the way. The image of the Heart of Jesus was everywhere in evidence, which fact was largely due to the Franciscan devotion to the Five Wounds and to the habit formed by the Jesuits of placing the image on the title-page of their books and the walls of their churches.

(6) Nevertheless, the devotion remained an individual or at least a private devotion. It was reserved to Blessed Jean Eudes (1602-1680) to make it public, to honour it with an Office, and to establish a feast for it. Père Eudes was above all the apostle of the Heart of Mary; but in his devotion to the Immaculate Heart there was a share for the Heart of Jesus. Little by little the devotion to the Sacred Heart became a separate one, and on 31 August, 1670, the first feast of the Sacred Heart was celebrated with great solemnity in the Grand Seminary of Rennes. Coutances followed suit on 20 October, a day with which the Eudist feast was thenceforth to be connected. The feast soon spread to other dioceses, and the devotion was likewise adopted in various religious communities. Here and there it came into contact with the devotion begun at Paray, and a fusion of the two naturally resulted.

(7) It was to Margaret Mary Alacoque (1647-1690), a humble Visitandine of the monastery at Paray-le-Monial, that Christ chose to reveal the desires of His Heart and to confide the task of imparting new life to the devotion. There is nothing to indicate that this pious religious had known the devotion prior to the revelations, or at least that she had paid any attention to it. These revelations were numerous, and the following apparitions are especially remarkable: that which occurred on the feast of St. John, when Jesus permitted Margaret Mary, as He had formerly allowed St. Gertrude, to rest her head upon His Heart, and then disclosed to her the wonders of His love, telling her that He desired to make them known to all mankind and to diffuse the treasures of His goodness, and that He had chosen her for this work (27 Dec., probably 1673); that, probably distinct from the preceding, in which He requested to be honoured under the figure of His Heart of flesh; that, when He appeared radiant with love and asked for a devotion of expiatory love—frequent Communion, Communion on the first Friday of the month, and the observance of the Holy Hour (probably June or July, 1674); that known as the "great apparition" which took place during the octave of Corpus Christi, 1675, probably on 16 June, when He said: "Behold the Heart that has so loved men . . . instead of gratitude I receive from the greater part (of mankind) only ingratitude . . .", and asked her for a feast of reparation on the Friday after the octave of Corpus Christi, bidding her consult Father de la Colombière, then superior of the small Jesuit house at Paray; and, finally, those in which solemn homage was asked on the part of the king, and the mission of propagating the new devotion was especially confided to the religious of the Visitation and the priests of the Society of Jesus. A few days after the "great apparition" of June, 1675, Margaret Mary made all known to Father de la Colombière, and the latter, recognizing the action of the spirit of God, consecrated himself to the Sacred Heart, directed the holy Visitandine to write an account of the apparition, and made use of every available opportunity discreetly to circulate this account through France and England. At his death, 15 February, 1682, there was found in his journal of spiritual retreats a copy in his own handwriting of the account that he had requested of Margaret Mary, together with a few reflections on the usefulness of the devotion. This journal, including the account and an excellent "offering" to the Sacred Heart, in which the devotion was well explained, was published at Lyons in 1684. The little book was widely read, even at Paray, although not without being the cause of "dreadful confusion" to Margaret Mary, who, nevertheless, resolved to make the best of it and profited by the book for the spreading of her cherished devotion. Moulins, with Mother de Soudeilles, Dijon, with Mother de Saumaise and Sister Joly, Semur, with Mother Greyfié, and even Paray, which had at first resisted, joined the movement. Outside of the Visitandines, priests, religious, and laymen espoused the cause, particularly a Capuchin, Margaret Mary's two brothers, and some Jesuits, among the latter being Fathers Croiset and Gallifet, who were destined to do so much for the devotion.

(8) The death of Margaret Mary, 17 October, 1690, did not dampen the ardour of those interested; on the contrary, a short account of her life published by Father Croiset in 1691, as an appendix to his book "De la Dévotion au Sacré Coeur", served only to increase it. In spite of all sorts of obstacles, and of the slowness of the Holy See, which in 1693 imparted indulgences to Confraternities of the Sacred Heart and, in 1697, granted the feast to the Visitandines with the Mass of the Five Wounds, but refused a feast common to all, with special Mass and Office, the devotion spread, particularly in religious communities. The Marseilles plague, 1720, furnished perhaps the first occasion for a solemn consecration and public worship outside of religious communities. Other cities of the South followed the example of Marseilles, and thus the devotion became a popular one. In 1726 it was deemed advisable once more to importune Rome for a feast with a Mass and Office of its own, but, in 1729, Rome again refused. However, in 1765, it finally yielded and that same year, at the request of the queen, the feast was received quasi-officially by the episcopate of France. On all sides it was asked for and obtained, and finally, in 1856, at the urgent entreaties of the French bishops, Pope Pius IX extended the feast to the Universal Church under the rite of double major. In 1889 it was raised by the Church to the double rite of first class. The act of consecration and of reparation were everywhere introduced together with the devotion. Oftentimes, especially since about 1850, groups, congregations, and States have consecrated themselves to the Sacred Heart, and, in 1875, this consecration was made throughout the Catholic world. Still the pope did not wish to take the initiative or to intervene. Finally, on 11 June, 1899, by order of Leo XIII, and with the formula prescribed by him, all mankind was solemnly consecrated to the Sacred Heart. The idea of this act, which Leo XIII called "the great act" of his pontificate, had been proposed to him by a religious of the Good Shepherd

# PREFACE

In 2014, my life was forever changed when
my wife, Rose, came home with our first
typewriter. I was in the throes of trying to
stay sober, unsuccessfully, and in the wake
of two miscarriages and finally the birth of
our third child, she received a Bipolar II
diagnosis. Different medications for her,
different ways to stay sober for me—nothing
seemed to be working the way we wanted it
to. But through writing and sharing our
respective journeys through typing and
sharing on social media, we found a release
and clarity neither of us had had before.
I assumed the role of "The Poetry Bandit"
to steal my love of writing back from my
addiction to alcohol. My wife went on to
write her way into remission with the help
of our doctor, therapy, and exercise. Today,
as you read this, I'm still sober, and this
book is a journey through the mending of my
broken heart during these last many years.

*Encyclopedia of a Broken Heart*, however, is
not just for people like me, but any person who
has suffered a brokenness they can't seem to
explain, whether at their own hands, someone
else's, or through no fault of their own. I am
eternally grateful to my Higher Power and all
of you who have lent their time, support and
readership to my journey. Thank you.

# ACTION

Retraction.
Distraction.
Hibernation.

Shards of heartache,
Splinters of my broken heart.

Shattered pieces like that one
Christmas ornament that finds
its way to the ground in fancy suicide.

Retraction.
Distraction.
Hibernation.

My heart desires
a lack of action.
It pulls apart so that
I cannot be put back
together easily.

Alone,
I hate it,
and yet it is a part
of me.

jon lupin

# AFTERLIFE

You have seen that white light,
and they call it your white life,
and I believe you.
I have seen it too, there,
so far
it's just too distant to be real.
But it is, you insist it is,
even though it only appears to me
like a pinhole star in the
dark sky of a future,
and that is
when it happens:
the afterlife will feel
as if the heartbreak was
only a puncture.

# AILING

A broken heart is not actually broken,
    but sick.

If you tell someone that you do not
    love them,
their heart still beats,
keeps them alive,
feeds the body.

But, it stops pumping blood
and starts pumping fear,
mistrust, conspiracy, experience.

If you break a promise,
the heart still beats,
keeps them alive,
feeds the body.

But, it stops pumping blood
and starts pumping fear,
mistrust, conspiracy, experience.

A broken heart is an ailing heart,
and yours will be no different.

jon lupin

# ALIEN

It is never pale.
It does not have big, black eyes.
No ship.
No mind probes.
No visitation from
the beyond.

It just feels like me,
because I have always felt
like I don't belong here,
an alien
watching all the
happy humans.

# ALONE

I hate it.
This word alone,
I hate more than
any other word
in my vocabulary.

I have a
murder of words,
and "alone" is the one
that shows up
time and time again.

Every page is,
full of words,
groups of phrases,
and cliques of meaning,
but full of loneliness.

# AMBIVALENT

Sit here.
Sit there.
Leave me.
Stay.

Take me on a walk through your heart.
Show me where the vines begin
and the flowers bloom.
Waltz with me through the
faded memories of your childhood.
Or not.
Close the path to your innermost being.
Let the vines recoil and your flowers fade.
Sit this one out while I wander what could
        have been a beautiful garden.

Ambivalent hearts
were broken once upon a time,
or still might be breaking.
So, don't worry about me.
I'll stick around until
it passes.

# BAIL

My hope is out on bail,
sprung surreptitiously
by my desire to one day be loved again.
The same hope
from when I first drew breath,
when I first drew
a picture of what I thought God looked
        like,
when I first came to realize
that the end was near,
but I continued to love you.

My hope is out on bail
and I just need a couple of bucks
to get by,
to find a job,
to find a place,
and start over.

# BATED

I fantasize about the breakup almost
    as often
as I fantasize about us lying together,
and I don't know what's wrong with me.

Well, it doesn't matter now.
My breath is bated for something to
    happen,
and I just don't know if
any of it is going to be for the best.

Maybe we just wait and see
what works and what doesn't?
Would that be so bad?

Maybe...

jon lupin

# BATTLE

My happiness wears
a bulletproof vest now.

I know stepping out
means war,
and I want
to ready myself for battle.

# BETTER

For her whole life,
people have been
calling her weird,
but the truth is,
her version of normal
is just better
than theirs.

# BETRAYAL

I write poems about you
with my eyes closed.
I can bear the
sight of the words
and the shape of the sentences,
but they find a way to
form themselves into
the shape your body
leaves behind in my bed.

It is easier on the eyes
if I am blind to your betrayal,
now, then, and every time I
grab a pen.

# BINGING

It's palpable,
the sinister sneakiness of sadness.
It's thick like a London fog,
sharp like the sarcasm on the tip
of a backbiter's tongue.

It blankets the floor
of where I like to lie,
binging on self-pity
and catastrophe.

While I lie here,
I will drink it all in
until the guilt starts to bloat,
settle in my gut,
and force me to face the fact
that I have failed myself again.

# BLESSING

It can get quite annoying,
when you're hurting,
to be told to look for the blessing
in the pain.

Let me just part the
Red Sea of tears
and look for the amazing shore
that awaits on the other side.
That's simply not possible,
at least not until
I'm sure I'm on dry ground.

# BREAKING

It can start as a hairline fracture,
just a word, or lack of attention,
or just a feeling that you have
    become banal
to the one who brings you joy.

It starts, and it doesn't stop—
a line growing slowly along the length
of the muscle that controls the fear,
that controls the anger.
It is the sadness you feel when you know
everything is about to end,
but somehow, you keep it together.

Breaking doesn't happen all the time
in a shattering speed.
Sometimes,
it can take a lifetime to completely
cause a person to fall apart.

# CAPABLE

It should never surprise you
what I'm capable of
when it comes to overcoming
the deepest cuts
to my ever-present heart.

As crazy as I might seem,
I'm just trying to
make sure
it looks good
sitting high up on my sleeve,
while looking down
upon the downtrodden fools
who tried and failed
to love you as
quixotically as I have.

# CARRIED

Sober now for
more days than
drunk,
and I always felt guilty
that I couldn't do it for you.

I carried guilt around
like yoke for the oxen,
or pillars for Samson.
I did it for me,
or at least that's what I tell people.

Deep down
I'm still trying to convince myself
everything I do clean
is for you,
and what I did as a drunk,
I did for me.

# CLANDESTINE

The heart gets
what the heart wants,
but it's always me,
cleaning up its mess.
I deserved better
than the clandestine feelings
of a muscle
gone mad
with power.

# CLANG

Nothing was more awkward
for me than the clinking of tea cups,
the clang of fork and knife,
pot and pan,
the grinding of teeth,
a grainy wash of
glances stolen across a table
I was sure would burst apart,
killing the lot of us
with wooden shards,
while waiting for you
to remember how
to greet me
with a kiss.

# CLARITY

In a moment
of clarity,
I knew you only ever
had to say
"I Love You"
once to keep me hooked.

It should have been
enough for me,
forever,
but it wasn't.

Obsession drew me in
like embers
in dark skies
on cold summer nights.

Before I loved you,
I wish I knew what
clarity meant, and
that it was an
eternal kind of thing.

# CLING

Yes, I'm clingy.
Yes, I'm needy.
And no, I'm not changing anytime soon.
I don't say that out of spite.

I cling
because I always feel like
I'm about to fall.

# COLD

Shattered,
like a teacup
in love with concrete.

Deaf,
like a heart
breaking with no sound.

Vanished,
like a love song written
in the water.

These disappointments all point to one
simple
cold,
hard,
fact:
The weight of doing anything
that must have meaning
is more than any one
can bear.

jon lupin

# COMPOSE

Put yourself together,
one piece at a time.

Marvel at how each time
you fall apart,
you build something
different, something stronger.

When you break apart each time
someone wants something from you
that you aren't prepared to give away,
you haven't let yourself crumble.

It's an ambush of the soul
and of the heart.
There's nothing to do
but to compose yourself,
give in to what you have learned,
and stand taller tomorrow.

# DAYS

The box I put myself in
is suddenly too small for me
and everything I still feel for you.
I am growing,
growing with discontent,
regret,
and a few other feelings I'm not sure
     about yet,
and it's getting uncomfortable in here.

You have shown me
what life is without walls,
what love sounds like out loud.
That fearing the next thing
is normal.

Life lived out there
amidst the uncertainty
will be better than a thousand days
in here.

# DEVASTATOR

What if I never come back?
What if this is it for
maniacal laughs and
brilliant bursts of creativity,
and the devastator of all truths?

The truth that I've become a zombie
obsessed with wanting to eat the
    brains
of those who wish only for peace and
    quiet?
What if I never come back to myself,
and I leave my poetry in the desert
like a scapegoat?

I don't know the answer,
and that scares me more than having
to be medicated for OCD
for the rest of my life.

# DIFFERENT

I went to the dark side
of beautiful
and came back
a different person.

# DISARMING

When I met you,
I didn't know where to look.
Your eyes were piercing.
Your smile, disarming.
Your skin, radiant.

The sound of your voice
was enough to make my heart
bleed through my skin,
a reminder
that I had been waiting for someone
who would kill
my loneliness.

# DOVE

My dove,
you only wanted to bring me peace,
a white flag
in a life
you could see was
fraught with
weapon and war.

# DRAMATIC

When you walk the other way,
the music in my head
becomes dramatic.
It's in a key and tempo
that lets me know
there's no way in hell
you'll be coming back.

# DREAM

I am haunted
by the shouts and the screams
of the dreams
I drowned with excuses
of not doing right by you.
But maybe
the second chance
I'm living right now
is the dream
that caught the life preserver.

# DULL

Your sharp edges
were all I needed
to soar this dull life
with my best mistakes.

jon lupin

# EARTHEN

Dry bones and desert skin
am I,
craving sweetness from the sky,
begging for a chance at life
once more.
Parched heart and barren soul
cry out for an oasis that will
bring relief.

To be earthen
is to wait out the drought,
hoping that when the
rains come,
I will drown in that
feeling of living
once more.

jon lupin

# ECHO

She has an
empty heart,
haunted by the ghost
of a voice
who once loved her,
ferociously,
vehemently,
without pause,
ever repeating the chorus
of a celebration
of two people
who sang together,
praised together,
kneeled together,
hoping
they would never become
each other's
echo.

# EFFORT

I am that
one painting on your wall
that is always crooked.
You don't bother to straighten me out.
I'm just there,
askew,
screaming out at all the other
items in your life
that seem to be in the
right places at all the right times.

I was put in this room for a reason
and it feels like you have forgotten why.
I used to illuminate this place
like a kaleidoscope
in the hands of a curious child
on a summer morning.

# ELECTRIC

A barrier of white, light blue
came between us,
our soul suddenly cleft.
It separated the conversation
between what was mundane
and what we were
supposed to discuss,
but whenever I tried,
up came the electric forcefield,
and I felt like
a breakthrough was never going
to happen.

I tried to be Moses,
a holy sledgehammer;
I even tried to scale this wall.
But no matter how I tried to cross
      your seas,
tear down your barriers,
and climb over your walls,
there would be no end to my labor.

So, outside your wall,
I bathe in pale blue
electric suspense,
knowing I will probably
die here.

# ELUSIVE

Elusive was the
wispy string of
consideration
I had tried
so very hard
to weave you
back into.
You were a needle
that would not be
threaded.

# EVIL

You let me know
with soft words, and soft fingers,
you were going to let me down
easy, gentle,
like a baby in a cradle
in a tree
that was rotten at the core.

It was pure evil
because you ended it,
and I felt like
it was the best thing
that had ever happened
to either of us.

I never knew I could
be broken
and feel so good
about it afterwards.

# FAULT

The fault between us
grew deeper and deeper,
creating an impasse
for which no bridge would do.
As the whites of your eyes
grew smaller
and the name from your lips
was muted by this chasm,
I was strangely attracted to
the idea
that I could be the one
to close the gap
with purposeful embraces
and a caress you would never forget.

Maybe if I had done this sooner –
maybe it wasn't me at all,
but it sure does feel like it
when you're on one side,
and I'm stuck with myself
on the other.

It's so easy to admit
that it was your fault
when you're talking to yourself.

# FEAR

Demons will always
have a fear
of
halos,
wings,
and the hearts
that go with them,
for they
will not
break easily.

# FIGURE

Life without you is a
figure in the dark,
a darkness that follows me
down every lit path,
enveloping all good things,
leaving the mark of the beast,
or what seems like a
dastardly deed that has yet
to be known.

It's a catastrophe
that hasn't happened yet,
but it's on repeat in my mind.
Every eye closed
is an admission that I know
it's an inevitability.

But,
one day,
I figure that spectre of losing you
will vanish,
and I'll be able to live
with my future again.

# FIRE

No one builds a fire
like you do.

No one
falls into it
like I do.

# FREEDOM

I miss freedom.
There are prisons all around me;
some I make myself,
and others you make for me.

I will always miss freedom
because I will always
need something to fight for.

# FURNACE

Nothing burns hotter than the
furnace in your heart
when the madmen play games,
and your love is on the line.

Their major crime was not loving you
with the zeal you deserved.
They handcuffed your dreams
and set them on fire in the streets,
letting everyone know you only loved
the bad boys.
This was the price.
But you weren't interested in
the value of a good kiss from a bad man,
you just wanted
to be valued,
and I was always showing up
with empty pockets.

# GALAXIES

It was never about the galaxies
or the universe,
or the starlight,
about what our horoscopes said,
or our unanswered prayers.
It was only ever about the
passion we had for each other
in the morning
and how we took advantage
of it before it dried up.

# GALLERY

To be a painted person,
sitting in the knotted frame
never leaving,
always still,
eyes fixed upon the place
where she likes to drink her tea.

This is what I desire most
now that I know she loves to paint,
and what I love the most is
she captured me just right.
My color. My hue.

The details in the wrinkles in
        my clothes;
the creases in my face,
the sadness in lights behind my eyes.
Every part of me in imperfect
perfection.

No one captured my sadness
like she did.
The guy in the gallery,
that's me,
and I'm not going anywhere.

# GAUNTLET

Nothing stings more than
the gauntlet of love,
backhanded across the face
when you least expected it.

Never fear,
with this pain, you will find purpose.
You'll bear the marks of a
beating you'll never forget:
a black eye to warn them
that your eyes tend to see
what they want;
a busted lip
to show them
that it's going to get bloody;
a crooked smile
to remind them that even though
you're in great pain,
you will manage to see
the best in them.

The fiercest lovers are those
who have survived
the harshest of times,
so, wear those scars
with pride.

jon lupin

# GHOSTLY

The greatest mistakes are
often the ones we
don't see coming.

You,
you have been
nothing but ghostly
since the first day we met.

I can see you,
yet I cannot hold you,
the glory in that love
that shimmers around
your form.
I cannot see a future
where I can hold you
and you can hold
anything more
than my gaze.

# GRAVITY

Buried slowly,
day by day,
in a grave
hollowed out by the
sheer weight
of my sins against
you.

The gravity of what
I had done
was not
what I had expected—
weightlessness
with a heavy heart.

jon lupin

# GUARDIAN

The last guardian
of your heart
ran from the fight
you didn't want to
face alone.

But you held the sword,
you held the shield,
you held their gaze
and became the
warrior you needed him to be.
He walked away
and you stepped into the fray.

Guard your own heart
and you will never be
fatally wounded.

# HANGOVER

You were my hangover cure,
until I realized that
you were drunk on loving
someone else,
and now that
bad taste in my mouth
is always there.

# HEADLONG

I look at old pictures of me,
and I can see that I used to smile
genuinely,
without fear that one day
it would crack
or that my teeth would yellow
from aging in a climate where it
was normal for people to blow smoke
into your face instead of up your ass.
I'm certain, though,
that if I keep smiling
headlong into a future
where I let go of my curious nature
to please the people who would
age me prematurely,
that everything will be okay,
and that my smile will
be white and happy once again.

# HEARTACHE

Heartache is a migraine,
pure and simple pain
that rocks your mind
with an intensity
that knows it will
come and go
until it puts you into a coma.
So, pop a pill if you must,
turn out the lights,
shut out the world,
shut out your family,
shut out your own self-worth,
shut out any notion that
it will pass without scarring
the inside of your eyes.
Heartache is a migraine,
pure and simple,
but remember,
it will pass.

# HELL

When the rain hits the hot pavement,
I am reminded that
everything I have experienced
starts off hot as hell
and that
relief follows
shortly after.

jon lupin

# IDENTITY

I fell in love with you
before I knew who I was.

I had
every chance to figure that out,
but I always knew I didn't love myself
    enough
to have an identity
that didn't involve
being loved by somebody else.
So, what's a guy to do
when he's been told that
his identity was stolen
by heartbreak?
I don't know,
but if you could tell me,
please do.

# ILLUSION

*Everything in moderation,*
is what they tell me.
Maybe you didn't have to drink
    that much.
Maybe you didn't have to fall that
    hard for her.
Maybe you didn't have to spend that
    much money.
It felt like a magic trick to me,
to do something without destroying
    myself.

I put myself into a gaping hole
until I understood that
I was able to climb out
and become a better person,
and that struggle
was not an illusion.

# IMMORTAL

I had a dream once that
I couldn't die.
My life kept rolling
over all the rest.
While they lived,
struggled,
celebrated,
danced,
cried,
mourned,
died,
I was always myself.

In the midst of it all,
wondering if my curse
would ever leave me—
was this immortal
desire to be the center of
their universe.

jon lupin

# INFLICTED

We were inflicted with a
need to be poisoned with this
toxin called love.
A beautiful vapor,
breathed in,
to transform us into
Romeo and Juliet,
Montague and Capulet,
taken too early to realize
love wasn't what
we needed.
It was good timing.

# INSPIRATIONAL

I have a hard time,
letting it go,
like all the songs and quotes
and inspirational posters
tell me I should
so that everyone around me
will be happy,
everyone will sigh
a great sigh of relief,
because I have let go of my anguish,
and they will then all be happy.
Yes, they will be happy.
Shouldn't I be the one to judge
when to let go?

# INVINCIBLE

I was walking through
an ineffable desire to be the one
who controlled every outcome.
I wanted to twist the fate doled out
to lovers like us,
but that is not what you wanted.
I just wanted us to be invincible,
But that could only happen
if I let my guard down.

# INVISIBLE

She wanted to be
invisible
just when he was home
because when he was home,
all he did,
all he saw
was her,
and she was never comfortable
being the apple
of his eyes.

# IOTA

Just one iota
of your love
was like an eternal
fountain,
always overflowing
with everything
I needed.

# JERICHO

Jericho will always fall.
No matter the brick,
no matter the mortar,
it will always fall.
No matter the memory,
no matter the hearts
that dwell inside for safety,
it will always fall.
No matter what you hide away,
no matter what secret you keep inside,
you will always fall.

So, let it go.
The truth will silence the feet;
it will silence the trumpets.

Jericho doesn't need to fall every time
we get together and try to have a
conversation.

# JOURNAL

They told me to write it down.
So I can stare at my worst fears,
scrawled hastily like a
prescription for a disease
that cannot be cured?
No.
I will not write it down
but rather,
I will live it,
for all to see
and for all to realize,
when you become a
walking journal,
there are some things
that should never be shared.

jon lupin

# JUSTIFY

You close your eyes
to justify how that
memory makes you feel:
Alone,
naked,
without breath,
nostalgic like missing that
warm blanket grandmother knit.
And you remember
crying over it when it was destroyed
by experiences too great
to feel in such a short frame.

All I want to do
is open your eyes,
do that heavy lifting,
and be there to show you
this new blanket I knit for you
with everything
I want for us.

# JUXTAPOSE

Today I feel black and white,
but tomorrow
I hope to be
technicolor.

jon lupin

# KARMA

Karma must have been
resting
when we were
kissing.

# KEEP

She's a keeper;
she's just not yours
to keep.

# KILLING

If the tears I cried
over you and what was lost
were currency,
I'd be making a killing.

# KNACK

Don't worry about me.
I'm fine.
This is fine.
Everything around me
is under a fine silt
of disappointment,
settling into a wet sand
of depression,
impressions of imprisonment
in the fact that I must
once again walk
this dirt road
alone.
But don't worry about me,
I've walked this road before
and I think I've finally got the knack
of not asking for help
from pretty eyes and
soft touches.

# KNEEL

I had to learn how to rebel
before I could learn how to kneel,
because I wasn't going to bow
to just anyone.
No, I would have bowed to you,
and you were the only one
who would have
accepted it as humility
and not as defeat.

# KNIT

See how it is?
Can't you see
how hard it is to forget someone?
How hard it is to live your life
as if they never were there,
never drinking the same tea,
never sharing the same bed,
never breathing the same
breath, inhaling the same air
while making it all one?
To move on,
to live your life
like you had never been
knit into another person
is about as difficult
as admitting
you were warm enough
not to have ever needed anyone
in the first place.

# LANGUAGE

Learning to speak
a language of love
that has no words,
only action,
only movement,
is what I wish to master
before I die.

# LIGHT

She wore light like a sweater,
putting it on
when she was lonely,
and taking it off
when she was hungry
for darkness.

jon lupin

# LIKENESS

You wanted this to work out,
and for a while,
it did just that. Worked out.
It had the likeness of something
    successful,
of something inspired by the greatest
moments in the romantic comedies
we used to watch until the early
    hours of the
next day,
under blankets and the hope
that in the morning
we would still be in love.

But,
I have been told that
love isn't something that
needs to work out,
it needs to be tended to
and never left alone
to figure itself out.

# LIVE

Darling,
don't let the trolls
bother you;
there's a reason why
they live under
bridges,
and you live
in the light.

# LOVE

Sometimes,
love is knowing
when to use a period
instead of a comma.

# LOVE POEMS

At the end of the day,
all we craved
was that all
the love poems
were going to be about us.

# MAGIC

I fall for you
like a child
falls for magic shows,
and though that
says more about me
than it does about you,
I will always be okay
with letting my
inner child
guide me to a
pure state of
happiness and
ignorance.

# MARK

Love your flaws
and learn from them.
They will make you aware
of what little time
we have left to
make our mark
before we're gone.

# MEMO

I'm sorry.
I wasn't aware that this seat
    was taken,
or that there was no longer
room in this heart for me.
I must have gotten my signals
    crossed, maybe.
Or I must have figured
our love was built of tougher stuff,
able to withstand
a life lived in slow motion.
I was happy.

I'm sorry,
but this isn't going to be easy.
My heart didn't get the memo.

jon lupin

# METTLE

I know sometimes
it looks dark out there,
that the light doesn't shine
as bright as it used to
or in the places that it needs to.
I know the steps
leading to the heavens
are fraught with cracks
and worn with traps;
this life is but a test of
your mettle, my dear,
and I'm going to need you
to pass with flying colors.

# MINGLE

I wanted you to meet me
in the space between
heart and soul,
that place inside
where the stars mingle
and make music,
where the galaxies shape shift
into the people we love
and love us back
and have our back;
that is where we should meet,
and not in some noisy bar.

# MOON

If I were to love you
to the moon,
would you stay there with me?

Would you help me
find the air to
speak one last word of love?

Would you abandon
all hope of going home,
to see the colors
life affords,
and stay there,
in the dust and crater,
the vacuum of a
broken heart,
just to love me?

If I were to love you
to the moon,
would you stay here with me?

# NEVER

You can build your walls
high around that city in your chest
and though you may
never call my name
when you need a hero
to save it,
I will not sleep
until I know your
heart is safe and
all your tears
are ones of joy.

Because that's what heroes do.

# NIGHTMARE

I fell asleep on the
sands of time,
a cruel place to take a nap,
and I cried aloud
with a voice that tore
the moment asunder.
I knew I had been left
alone,
left for dead,
where everything stood still
and it forced me to
realize I had two options:

Beat down this lonely, granular
    nightmare
and wake up to live again,
or go back to sleep,
lost in loneliness,
and with sand
in every crack
of my broken heart.

jon lupin

# NOTHING

When I am left
with nothing
but leftovers
at a table you left long ago,
maybe I will finally
understand the price
of asking for more
than I can handle.

# NUISANCE

Walk with me,
won't you?
My road is long and
unforgiving;
having someone to
share it with
makes the unkindness
of ravens
who follow me
less of a nuisance
and more of a
choir.

jon lupin

# OATH

Don't make me promise
that this will all work out.
This is an oath
I cannot make,
but trust me,
it is not one that I would break
either,
if it should lie upon the table
beside your cutting board
and sharp knife
of decision.
I would offer any limb
in place of such a promise,
but instead,
I would ask you to love
my trust as you love my face.

jon lupin

# OBSESSION

Deep within the farthest reaches
of my soul
is a place I keep clean and tidy
just for her.
It's a place
she could call home
if that is what she desires,
a place where she can
focus her obsessions
in one thought,
one dream,
one name,
which is hopefully mine.

# OKAY

You don't need anyone to tell you
what to worry about,
and you don't need anyone
telling you to stop frowning,
feeling, furrowing that brow.
What you do need to be told,
everyday,
is that "It's okay"
and
"We love you
no matter what."

# OMINOUS

It only seems that way,
to be in a room,
a safe place,
somewhere I can hang my hat
and pet my dog,
curl up with a blanket
and watch my
favorite show.
But to do this
or to start my week
without your touch,
seems ominous to me.
So, I'll float
through that terrifying reality
until you come back
and bring that anchor.

# ONE

Do not be
a one-line poem,
be the whole book.

Do not be
one link,
be the whole chain.

Do not be
one thought,
be the whole philosophy.

Do not be
one drop,
be the deluge.

# OUTCAST

We were weak.
We went places
we shouldn't have gone.
We played roles
we weren't suited to play.
We were stubborn.
We ate poison
when we should
have chosen food,
but then again,
we were outcasts
and nothing we were
going to do
was ever going to bring us
into the fold again.

# PAST

The problem with the past
is that it knows
where I am the most
ticklish.
It continues to creep up
behind me and
jab its bony fingers
into my sides
or into my feet,
thinking
that trying to make me
laugh about my mistakes
is a good idea.

# PERFECT

I never asked to be
preached to
by a perfect person,
just a fighting
and honest one.

jon lupin

# PICNIC

Nothing about this was easy.
Not the praying,
not the hellos,
not the cringing every time
I wanted to talk things out,
not the breathing when we
felt ourselves getting too close
    too soon.
Everything was "too soon"
and it drove me mad.
All I wanted to do was raise my flag
and claim this love as our own again,
but you were hesitant,
always wary about the repercussions
of banging that drum too loud.

Well, it doesn't matter anyway
because I can wait.
You made ruin
feel like a picnic.

# PIECES

It's there. Everywhere.
The expression that
you are broken,
that you need to heal.

We are all in the same boat,
just a bunch of
broken vases trying to be passed off
as okay-enough in
the world's antique store.

If we add up our broken pieces,
we are still a whole person
and the glue
should be each other.

# PRAY

We cannot be
set free
from the same pain
we pray for.

Be careful what you wish for.

# PRETENDING

The hardest part of being
without you
is knowing when to
stop pretending you're still here.

# QUALITY

I have often thought about the
quality of my pain and suffering,
how it is the finest kind there is,
and how it shines when you
hold it up to the light.
It sounds perfectly hollow
when you tap on it;
it bounces back when
you hit it.

No sir, you won't find pain and suffering
quite like this
no matter where you look
on God's green earth.

It's all mine,
and I don't feel like
sharing it with anyone today.
Sometimes,
it's okay to be selfish.

# QUEEN

She could be bruised.
She could be cut.
She could bleed.
She could be
put under by a broken world.
And still,
she would heal,
dust herself off,
and tell you
she will be okay,
because she is a queen
and she is built of
tougher stuff.

# QUIT

My heart is eager,
but my flesh
wishes to quit
while there's still time,
time to find a way out
before it's too late,
before there's nothing
left to do but
skin myself alive
and show you
who I truly am.
Trust me,
there is nothing
scarier than showing
someone I love
how I have not been loved.

# QUOTATION

I write in the morning now,
because when the
rising sun hits your
skin through the open window,
well,
I could write a whole
book about how
beautiful that is.

# REALIZE

Do you see it?
Look a little closer,
there, past the skin,
the tissue,
the sinew,
the muscle,
the veins and arteries,
blood and cells,
in between the parts of
my DNA.

It's a feeling,
hiding deep behind
my soul,
and it was you
who made me realize
what it was.

I am enough
and you loved me for it.

# REBELS

If you want to learn
how to love
selflessly,
look for the rebels;
the rebels
will teach you
sacrifice.

jon lupin

# REMIND

I dream of a day
when the blossoms
stay as they are—
a colorful cloud of pink and white.
Rays of sunshine upon it, casting
patterns of haphazard happiness.
It's a delicate array of shimmering
    laughter
caught by a breeze,
but the blossoms do not fall to
    the ground.

If they could stay as they were
and not remind me that the
season must change,
this would ease my mind
and hold off a cold creeping
that culminates in summer,
a season that stifles me,
reminds me
of the heartbreak that is sure to follow.

# REVEALING

When I emerge from the darkness,
I wish to be free of the sludge
weighing heavy upon my limbs.
I want to be free of the moniker,
the pseudonym,
the shadows of my doubts
who have lingered here too long.
I want to be rid of all of it,
and when my time is right,
I'll step out into the light
and dress my heart
in a sexy little number,
something bold
but not too revealing.

jon lupin

# RIGHTEOUS

Here,
with the lame,
the tilted,
the off-kilter,
the ones you call crazy,
the far from home,
the addicted,
the broken pieces of humans
you once felt comfortable around,
this is where I find a place
to sit.
Free of righteous indignation,
and all together,
holding hands in a circle,
just trying to make
sense of life
instead of trolling our way through.

# RULES

As I heal,
people have come to me
with the kindest intentions,
but with a glint in their eye
that this sadness
is all for them.
What they don't know
is that I can see it coming;
their advice, it is really a
remote control they use
to rewind their own sadness.

Too many rules
for my body
and nothing
for my heart.

Let me heal in peace,
because the quiet
is where I keep
who I am.

jon lupin

# SAINT

Weep not for the sinner,
but cry your trenches full
for the saint
who has no fear
of himself.

jon lupin

# SEEKING

Gaunt, but nimble enough
to take a jaunt down
memory lane and see what
I left behind when I was just
trying to get out of your way
when you were mad.
All I found there
were wounds,
unhealed by an excess of
salt left behind by a sneer,
a comment,
a word I have never ever
forgotten.

So, what am I doing here?
I'm seeking forgiveness,
but not from you,
from my old self.
I came here
to my past,
to give myself a break
and to remind myself
you are not worth
remembering.

# SELF-LOVE

It's everywhere these days,
the constant reminder
that I must love myself first
before I can learn how to love
another human being.
And while I see the wisdom in this,
I also see that this could be
my easy way out
from dealing with my past,
my mistakes,
my need for resolution.
Everyone is selling self-love tactics
to get rich so they can love themselves
into a sweet new ride or a hot pair of
    shoes,
but have they ever followed up
to see if their words work?
I don't think so.
So, instead,
I think I'll get my affairs in order,
find you,
apologize,
humble myself,
and clean the slate,
because I feel,
only then
will I be able to love myself
and do it better than some
internet guru could sell.

jon lupin

# SKY

Come,
find me
on the other side
of crazy,
where the sky is
darker than normal,
and where the lost
have come to die.

# SNAKE

You can be
my spouse,
my lover,
my best friend,
my friend,
my acquaintance,
my boss,
my co-worker,
my sponsor,
my therapist,
my stranger,
my guardian angel,

but please,
do not be
the snake.

jon lupin

# SUMMER'S DAY

Wings of silver,
a heart of gold,
bronze skin
and sapphire eyes;
on a summer's day
you always felt
like treasure.

# TALE

Show me a life
without worry and
I will follow you
until the end of my days.
And when I do pass,
I'll pass into the lore
and grace the tall tales.
I will tell the spirits and the saints
it was you
who saved my life
after I lived it.

# TATTOO

One day,
I'll write something
someone will tattoo
somewhere on their body,
and when that happens,
I will be immortal,
at least until that person dies.
But until then,
I'll be happy with
your eyes
etching these poems
into the back of your
mind.

# THUNDER

Without you,
I'm like thunder
with no lightning;
just a whole lot
of noise
and nothing to show
for it.

# TOMORROW

Tomorrow is going
to be hard.
It will try to run you down,
and if you aren't careful
it will get your little dog, too.
So, be strong,
and hold on to that
leash nice and tight.
Let the demons know
you won't go down without a fight,
and your angels
that you aren't ready
to hand in that pink slip
just yet.

# TORTUROUS

Love is a
terror when it is
not muzzled,
when it has not fed
in some time.
It is insatiable when it
gets its first taste
of fresh flesh in
the pale moonlight
on a midsummer's eve.
It will bite and scream,
howl with you
or silence your softest whisper;
it will show you pleasure
or it will give you pain.

Love is a torturous
thing,
isn't it?

# TREMBLED

"I just wanted more," he sighed
     heavily.

"But," she trembled,
"there is nothing left to give.
You have it all."

If everything you have
in your heart is not enough,
find someone who doesn't
crowd their basket
with themselves and what
they want.

jon lupin

# UNCANNY

It was uncanny
how you were able
to show me that
the past should be
an open book,
so that you can go back
and find where
it all went wrong,
and where it started
to go right.
Isn't it odd
that I should always
find your name
mentioned in that page?

# UNFURL

A good time to believe in yourself
is when you're lying on the
ground, fallen fighters
strewn around you,
their unlived dreams spilling
upon the gray grass,
screaming and dying,
seeping into the cold,
unforgiving earth.
Yours are still alive
for a reason.
Get up,
unfurl your battle flag,
grab your dreams and
plunge headlong
into the forces
that would have you die,
just like every other
person who gave up
their chance at happiness.

# UNIQUE

There was nothing new
about the way this wound healed.
It closed up
just like all the others.
The scar was similar
to those received
from the ones who tried
loving me with a pure heart
but couldn't handle the
darkness dripping from mine.

I named it,
gave it a date,
wrote it down,
typed up a poem,
and put it in my pocket,
waiting for the next time
someone would hurt me.

And I guess that's what makes
me unique—
not the fact that I've been hurt,
but that no matter
how many times it happens,
I'm hoping that the
new wound is deep enough
for me to bury
that poem in it.

jon lupin

# UNISEX

Love is blind
to the status of my heart,
is blind to the
color of my mood.
Love heeds no
instruction,
comes with no instructions,
deconstructs every
construct the mind may
create to house it in.

Love is unisex
and does not discriminate
when it arrives
and when it leaves.
Love is the politician
who does the perfect job
and begs no praise,
and when it's gone,
all you can do is think
about how great it was
to have someone who
didn't judge you,
just accepted you.

# UPSWING

I won't lie.
There have been a lot of
tears shed,
a lot of whining,
moaning,
complaining,
pejorative phrases murmured
in hopes pity would
throw me a party,
a party everyone forgot about,
a party where there's only
one song playing,
and it's some swing-band tune
everybody is dancing to
somewhere I wasn't invited.

But that's okay,
I'm on the upswing, baby.
I've got my dancing shoes on
at a party for one
and I just kicked pity out
for spiking my drink,
knowing full well
I'm sober now.

# USURP

Inside this Trojan horse
I hide,
waiting for the perfect moment
to spring my trap
of love unfurled
in the winds of change,
to flay doubt,
to spread the terror of
my heart across the land
and usurp the throne.
Hate has stolen
from those of us
who just wanted to
love each other in
the peace and quiet
of a glen now misted
with the blood
of our generation.

When we are victorious
we will love again,
but until then,
it's just bow and arrow,
sword and shield,
blood and heart,
you and me.

# VALENTINES

She wishes,
that for just once in her life,
she would receive
valentines
from her angels
instead of from
her demons.

# VAMPIRES

Blood will always
course through us,
making us visible and tasty
for the vampires
who live under
our beds,
in our closets,
and in our school desks,
in our phones,
in our dreams,
in the bedeviled little places
we keep secret from our parents,
in the space between the heart
and the soul.

The harder we try to hide,
the more visible we become,
so, it might be best
to just be out with it.

jon lupin

# VANDAL

She was a happy
little vandal,
smashing opinions
in the street
and setting fire
to your heart.

# VELOCITY

How do you calculate
the velocity of a
broken heart?

I was on cloud nine,
then rag-dolled to the ground,
at a speed which caused
this heart to
crumble and
shatter any record
in a high school science book.

Write that out
and I will tell you
if this is how it felt
when you walked away.

# VERSION

What would you like today?
What suits your mood?
Should I not speak today?
Stand over here, and nod
when I come up in conversation,
or should I rise up
over all the rules,
all the pomp and circumstance
you like to
usher in before me?
Should I tell them about
my version of how
we met,
how you introduced me to
silence,
a cage,
and hung around my neck
a sign saying,
"I am the version of
what is most palatable
to people who don't really care."

I think it's time
I told the stories around here
because I am tired
of being mute.

# VEST

Invest a little
in yourself;
get yourself started
with some basic happiness.
When you have that,
weaponize it.
Get yourself a scope.
Calibrate.
When you're satisfied,
get yourself some ammo,
a few memories
to load up with,
ones that make you smile,
stockpile that.
Get more than you need.
In fact, get enough
to arm an entire army of
like-minded people.
Then,
open your door and
wait for the war to come your way.

But you'll be alright,
because you were smart,
you're armed,
and your happiness
wears a bulletproof vest.

jon lupin

# WAITS

Time waits
for no one
but you waited for me,
and that's all
that mattered.

# WEIGH

You know it's time
for you to get out of your head
and into your heart
when life begins
to weigh
too much.

# WHISKEY

This is not a poem
about whiskey, nor is it about
getting drunk on words—
in fact,
if anything,
my words are the exact opposite.

They are a sobering truth,
a testament to the world
that a life lived
skinny dipping into
whiskey glasses,
slurred words and
incomprehensible stories
lead nowhere but
an empty book,
pages stripped of meaning.

This poem is definitely
not about whiskey;
it's different than all the others,
because I'm not drunk
and my words
won't sting and leave
you with a headache.

# WHITEWASHED

I like to people-watch
when I'm not feeling
all that good about myself.
So many people,
not realizing I'm sitting there,
half judgmental,
half empathetic,
but it sure is easier to be
thankful for my colorful past
when watching all the
whitewashed souls
trudge slowly by.

# WICK

With candles lit,
we gave of each other
until the wicks burned out
and the wax covered
our wicked little wanderings.

# WON

You are not a loser.

You just haven't won
the right battle yet.

# X

You were a national treasure
never wanting to be buried,
never wanting to be simply marked
with an X.

# XEROX

Nothing is more frustrating
than putting all your effort into
something,
such as writing a book,
building a house,
setting a table for two,
breaking a habit,
drowning a feeling,
starting to love,
only to have that Xerox
of your latest heartbreak
hanging in the peripheraly,
reminding you that
failure is a possibility.

But today,
I'll choose to remember
that I also learned lessons,
and that piecing together
a broken heart
satisfied my
OCD
and that I love a good puzzle.

# YEARN

Homegrown love,
the kind that makes you think
of soft summer nights,
sparklers fizzing out in supple hands,
singeing flesh,
stinging fresh,
feeling like you were invincible
and that the stolen kisses
at parties were
more valuable than gold.
We yearn for summer like
we strive for perfection,
and it shows on your neck,
your lips and your hips.

# YEARS

We tried to put space
between us,
and we were foolish enough
to think that years
spent not thinking about each other
would really heal the wounds
around the knives
we left in each other's backs
after that long and awkward embrace.
Do you remember
how long it took to walk away
after that cold human lock?
It felt longer than the years
we spent hiding
in plain sight from one another.
I hated not having
the key to forgiving you
and still living with my pain
in case you did not feel the same way.
I guess this is the danger
in putting years
in a place where we should have put
kindness.

# YES

What your heart needs
to hear occasionally
is "no."
"Yes" can be poison for the soul,
a comfort that the world
will not happily bestow
upon anyone
wishing for the easy way
out of every
awkward situation.

# YET

I wasn't enough,
and yet,
you couldn't let me go.
It was believing in heaven
as a back-up plan
when your personal hell
was too much bear.
It was when the reality hit
that maybe there was
something more to life
than just a quick kiss and
brush of the cheek,
a hug in darkness that lasted
longer than
winter's dark blanket.

I was never enough,
and yet,
you couldn't let me go,
but you should,
because I can't save you.

# YIELD

When your heart is
on the mend,
wolves will come,
vultures will circle above you,
predators who dress like prey
will reveal pointed fang.
The voices who once rang
out with libertarian sounds
will enslave
you to their will and have you
remain lame,
dependent upon nothing but
the thought that this might be
your last love.

Never yield,
never give them the satisfaction
of seeing your flesh
pressed upon your ribs,
but let them see the
flame behind your eyes,
and fists clenched.
Do not go down without a fight,
and your heart will
beat twice as strong as it did
before.

jon lupin

# YOKE

I once told you
a burden is never heavy
if it's shared with
someone who cares,
but the yoke this ache
puts upon my heart
is one that
should be carried alone.
It was I who made it
as heavy as it has become.

# YOU

You were the kind of woman
who cured my writer's block.

You were not the one,
you were the only one.

# YOUNG

Nothing stirs the heart more than
the chance to feel young again,
and nothing made me feel like that
like the first time we held hands.
Broken hearts
are often older hearts,
having been through more,
aging at an alarming pace,
and mine was no different.
When I met you,
it was like drinking from the
fountain lost to tales
only children had the
courage to believe in anymore.

# ZEALOT

Harlot or zealot?
No one was quite sure
what I had become,
always dancing,
always singing,
always drunk and oblivious
to how desperate I was
for the attention of others.
But now,
I can see,
I was only trying to embrace
my flaws,
because they reminded me
how little time I had left
to make my mark.

# ZENITH

I wrap myself
with a zodiac of stars,
and though I'm not one to put
any weight behind it,
it seems to put some weight
upon my body,
and I can look to the
zenith and feel a power
telling me that everything
is going to be okay,
one day at a time,
one heartbeat at a time,
if those minuscule moments
are free of booze, self-loathing
and resentment.
I can start here,
under a clear sky
before God and many witnesses
and live a sober life,
one that you can be proud of,
one that will help you
mend that heart of yours
and the damage I caused.

# ZERO

I have no regrets.
I have no doubts
that this story of mine
is told every day,
and that everyone who hears it
wonders how is it possible
that a heart under so much weight
has the strength to beat
hard enough to force the chest to rise
    above?
I have zero compulsions
to add more stones to this altar
that life tried to burn me on
many years ago,
and with that I will make sure
that my words are light,
my gaze is airy
and my heart continues
to be a firm foundation
on which to rebuild my life.

# ZIGZAG

Trace that delicate finger
down my back,
zigzag through the crests
of my backbone,
through the cracks and
bridges time has worn into it.
Apply some pressure
and scratch what I cannot reach:
that feeling that
something wicked no longer
comes for me
and my life is now
as comfortable as our bed.

jon lupin

# ZOMBIE

Near the end of our lives
there's a strange opportunity
to breathe new love
into an old life.
It is a love that will last long
into your afterlife,
a place where your mind
will be old
and your body new—
a reverse zombie
full of life
and a desire to love
without knowledge of
death,
or that it was a
broken heart that put
you in the ground.

# ABOUT THE POET

Jon Lupin is a writer and father. He shares his stories of love, healing, and restoration the best way he knows how: with poetry. Jon lives in the suburbs of Vancouver, Canada, with his three children and his dog. You can find him on his popular Instagram account @The_PoetryBandit.